POSITIVE MINDSET JOURNAL

for

SPECIAL EDUCATION TEACHERS

A Year of Happy Thoughts, Inspirational Quotes, and Reflections for a More Rewarding Special Education Teaching Experience

Grace Stevens

Copyright 2018 by Grace Stevens

No part of this publication may be reproduced or transmitted in any form or by any means, mechanical or electronic, including photocopying or recording, or by any information storage and retrieval system, or transmitted by email without permission in writing from the publisher.

Paperback Edition

ISBN: 978-0-998 7019-5-0

Manufactured in the United States of America

All Rights Reserved

Red Lotus Books
Mountain House CA

This journal belongs to:

_____

School Year: _____

For Josh and all his teachers – inside and outside the classroom

A TEACHER AFFECTS ETERNITY; HE CAN NEVER TELL WHERE HIS INFLUENCE STOPS.

— *Henry B. Adams* —

How To Use This Book

Teaching is a "noble" career. We chose it because we knew it was important, not because we thought it would be easy. This is especially true of Special Education. While dedicating your professional life to serving the most vulnerable of students can be the most rewarding endeavor, it can also be the most challenging. Few people truly understand how genuinely unmanageable the workload can be and the vast spectrum of responsibilities that it encompasses. The amount of meetings and paperwork involved is overwhelming and can often feel like it has little to do with what we want to truly focus on - connecting with students, advocating for them, and making a positive impact on their lives. While we may have little control of the mandates and policies in education, we do have control over the positive energy that we bring to our students and our classroom every day. This latter area is where this journal can help.

The goal of this journal is to help you connect to the parts of your teaching week that bring you joy. While there is plenty of research to support the idea that a positive classroom environment will increase student engagement and achievement, this journal isn't for your students' benefits; it's for yours. You deserve to enjoy your teaching day!

Many years of experience in the classroom have taught me that everyone's day goes smoother when the teacher is happy. I have also learned that there are specific things that I can do to train my mind to focus on the "good stuff", seek out opportunities to make a student's, a parent's or a co-worker's day and remind myself of how awesome a privilege it really is to spend my day with special needs children.

This journal is designed to help you take a few moments to reflect on your intentions before the work week gets rolling and its momentum gets you into "survival mode." How will you take care of your needs? Who can you celebrate? Who can you thank?

Taking a few minutes to write down the best parts of your day before you go home will put you in a better mental space and train your mind to be a "Joy Detective," focusing on looking for positive aspects in your day. Teaching special education can be isolating. School-wide recognition programs usually celebrate academic achievement or benchmarks that may simply not be attainable for some of your students. General education teachers may not understand what a huge victory it can be for one of your students to go a day (a morning, an hour) without a behavior or mastering a task that others take for granted. You have to be your own champion. Making note of small wins and moments of joy can help. Science shows that training your brain to seek out things you are grateful for and inspired by is simply a habit. If you work on flexing your "happy muscle" daily, you will find it easier to connect to joy in your day and share that joy with others.

Three weeks is all it takes to form a new habit. Leave this journal on your desk and resolve to make writing in it a daily practice. It will help put you in a positive mindset daily and, at the end of the year, you will also have a keepsake of a window in time that you shared with a unique group of students.

I hope this journal helps you connect to the moment and find more joy in your day and your classroom.

What you do matters! I thank you for your dedication from the bottom of my heart. Make it a great year!

Grace

P.S. This journal is a companion piece to a book I wrote called <u>Positive Mindset Habits for Teachers - 10 Steps to Reduce Stress, Increase Student Engagement and Reignite Your Passion for Teaching</u>. You can use this journal as a stand-alone piece, but if you are serious about transforming your teaching, I think you will enjoy the book too. You can find it on Amazon and at happy-classrooms.com

Focus - Connect to Your 'Why'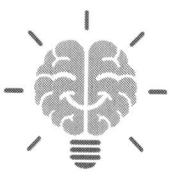

Why did you decide to become a Special Education teacher?

_____

_____

_____

_____

_____

_____

Who were some of the key people who inspired you to this path?

_____

_____

_____

What did you hope to achieve when you first started teaching Special Ed?

_____

_____

_____

_____

Focus - Success Stories

LIST the top lives you have positively influenced as a Special Education teacher. Think beyond students and remember that you have positively impacted the lives of parents, caregivers and entire families, as well as colleagues.

1. _____
2. _____
3. _____
4. _____
5. _____
6. _____
7. _____
8. _____
9. _____
10. _____

On the days when you are feeling overwhelmed and under-appreciated, look back at this list and remember that what you do MATTERS.

Beginning of Year Intentions

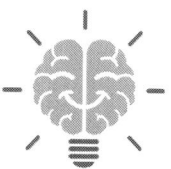

What are some ways I can ensure my students and I have the most positive classroom experience this year?

_____

_____

_____

_____

_____

_____

Some things I already do that I love and should KEEP

_____

_____

_____

Some things that would be helpful to CHANGE

_____

_____

_____

Some things that would be helpful to START

_____

_____

_____

_____

_____

What are some things I love doing *outside* of school that I can commit to engaging in to ensure I stay energized, excited about teaching, and happy in general?

_____

_____

_____

_____

_____

_____

_____

_____

_____

Support System

Who is going to be my "life line" in my professional life this year? Who is the person I can rely on for input, advice, a shoulder to lean on, my "safe place," or just someone to laugh and celebrate with?

_____

_____

Who will be the "life lines" in my personal life?

_____

_____

_____

Which colleague or colleagues can I develop a closer relationship with this year? (Can I be someone's life line?)

_____

_____

_____

_____

Notes from Professional Development

What "take aways" do I have from the beginning of the year Professional Development? Which ideas can I immediately implement before they get forgotten? Which ones in particular might contribute to a more joyful classroom experience?

_____

_____

_____

_____

_____

_____

_____

_____

_____

_____

_____

_____

_____

Notes from Professional Development

_____
_____
_____
_____
_____
_____
_____
_____
_____
_____
_____
_____
_____
_____

You are **VALUED**. What you do every day **MATTERS**. Let's rock this year!

> *"Every student can learn, just not on the same day, or in the same way."*
>
> - John Evans

Date _____

My intention for this week:

_____

_____

_____

Who I can champion this week:

_____

Ways I Can Take Care of **Myself** and **My Students** This Week:

- ☐ 1. _____

- ☐ 2. _____

- ☐ 3. _____

The best three parts of today or "wins" my students had: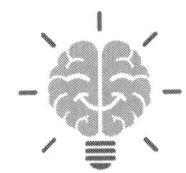

Monday:

1. _____

2. _____

3. _____

Tuesday:

1. _____

2. _____

3. _____

Wednesday:

1. _____

2. _____

3. _____

The best three parts of today or "wins" my students had:

Thursday:

1. _____
2. _____
3. _____

Friday:

1. _____
2. _____
3. _____

Something I am especially grateful for this week:

_____
_____
_____

Quote of the Week: (funniest thing a student said, a compliment you were given, or something inspirational you read)

Three people I can **thank** or **celebrate** this week - in person, in writing, or by making a "day maker" phone call, text or e-mail.

- _____ ☐
- _____ ☐
- _____ ☐

Check as you complete ✓

The most **productive meeting** I was involved in this week and what I hope its impact will be:

_____
_____
_____
_____
_____

> *" What most people don't know is that most Special Education teachers are really angels disguised as extraordinary humans."*
>
> - Joe Martin

Date _____

My intention for this week:

_____

_____

_____

Who I can champion this week:

_____

Three Ways I Can Take Care of **Myself** and **My Students** This Week:

- [ ] 1. _____
- [ ] 2. _____
- [ ] 3. _____

The best three parts of today or "wins" my students had: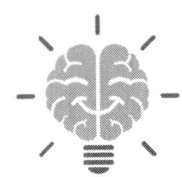

Monday:

1. _____
2. _____
3. _____

Tuesday:

1. _____
2. _____
3. _____

Wednesday:

1. _____
2. _____
3. _____

The best three parts of today on "wins" my students had:

Thursday:

1. _____
2. _____
3. _____

Friday:

1. _____
2. _____
3. _____

Something I am especially grateful for this week:

_____
_____
_____

Quote of the Week: (funniest thing a student said, a compliment you were given, or something inspirational you read)

Three people I can **thank** or **celebrate** this week - in person, in writing, or by making a "day maker" phone call, text or e-mail.

- _____ ☐
- _____ ☐
- _____ ☐

Check as you complete ✓

The most **productive meeting** I was involved in this week and what I hope its impact will be:

_____
_____
_____
_____
_____

> *"Every kid is one caring adult away from being a success story."*
>
> - unknown

Date _____

My intention for this week:

_____

_____

_____

Who I can champion this week:

_____

Three Ways I Can Take Care of **Myself** and My **Students** This Week:

- [ ] 1. _____
- [ ] 2. _____
- [ ] 3. _____

The best three parts of today or "wins" my students had:

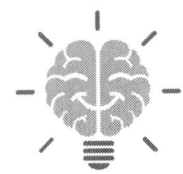

Monday:

1. _____

2. _____

3. _____

Tuesday:

1. _____

2. _____

3. _____

Wednesday:

1. _____

2. _____

3. _____

The best three parts of today or "wins" my students had: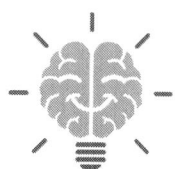

Thursday:

1. _____
2. _____
3. _____

Friday:

1. _____
2. _____
3. _____

Something I am especially grateful for this week:

_____
_____
_____

Quote of the Week: (funniest thing a student said, a compliment you were given, or something inspirational you read)

Three people I can **thank** or **celebrate** this week - in person, in writing, or by making a "day maker" phone call, text or e-mail.

- _____ ☐
- _____ ☐
- _____ ☐

Check as you complete ☑

The most **productive meeting** I was involved in this week and what I hope its impact will be:

_____
_____
_____
_____
_____

> *"Everybody is a genius. But if you judge a fish by its ability to climb a tree, it will live its whole life believing that it is stupid."*
>
> - Albert Einstein

Date _____

My intention for this week:

_____

_____

_____

Who I can champion this week:

_____

Three Ways I Can Take Care of **Myself** and **My Students** This Week:

- 1. _____
- 2. _____
- 3. _____

The best three parts of today or "wins" my students had: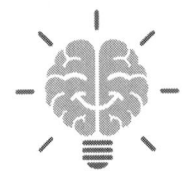

Monday:

1. _____

2. _____

3. _____

Tuesday:

1. _____

2. _____

3. _____

Wednesday:

1. _____

2. _____

3. _____

The best three parts of today or "wins" my students had: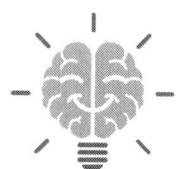

Thursday:

1. _____

2. _____

3. _____

Friday:

1. _____

2. _____

3. _____

Something I am especially grateful for this week:

_____
_____
_____

Quote of the Week: (funniest thing a student said, a compliment you were given, or something inspirational you read)

Three people I can **thank** or **celebrate** this week - in person, in writing, or by making a "day maker" phone call, text or e-mail.

- _____
- _____
- _____

Check as you complete ☑

The most **productive meeting** I was involved in this week and what I hope its impact will be:

_____
_____
_____
_____
_____

> "Act as if what you do makes a difference.
> It does".
> - William James

Date _____

My intention for this week:

_____

_____

_____

Who I can champion this week:

_____

Three Ways I Can Take Care of **Myself** and **My Students** This Week:

- ☐ 1. _____
- ☐ 2. _____
- ☐ 3. _____

The best three parts of today or "wins" my students had: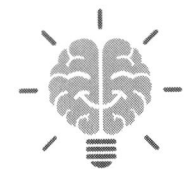

Monday:

1. _____

2. _____

3. _____

Tuesday:

1. _____

2. _____

3. _____

Wednesday:

1. _____

2. _____

3. _____

The best three parts of today or "wins" my students had:

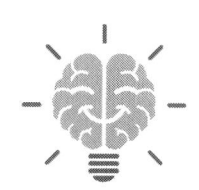

Thursday:

1. _____

2. _____

3. _____

Friday:

1. _____

2. _____

3. _____

Something I am especially grateful for this week:

_____

_____

_____

Quote of the Week: (funniest thing a student said, a compliment you were given, or something inspirational you read)

Three people I can **thank** or **celebrate** this week - in person, in writing, or by making a "day maker" phone call, text or e-mail.

- _____ ☐
- _____ ☐
- _____ ☐

Check as you complete ☑

The most **productive meeting** I was involved in this week and what I hope its impact will be:

_____
_____
_____
_____
_____

> *"It is easier to build strong children than to repair broken men. "*
>
> - Frederick Douglas

Date _____

My intention for this week:

_____
_____
_____

Who I can champion this week:

_____

Three Ways I Can Take Care of **Myself** and **My Students** This Week:

- ☐ 1. _____
- ☐ 2. _____
- ☐ 3. _____

The best three parts of today or "wins" my students had:

Monday:

1. _____

2. _____

3. _____

Tuesday:

1. _____

2. _____

3. _____

Wednesday:

1. _____

2. _____

3. _____

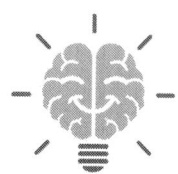

The best three parts of today or "wins" my students had:

Thursday:

1. _____

2. _____

3. _____

Friday:

1. _____

2. _____

3. _____

Something I am especially grateful for this week:

_____

_____

_____

Quote of the Week: (funniest thing a student said, a compliment you were given, or something inspirational you read)

Three people I can **thank** or **celebrate** this week - in person, in writing, or by making a "day maker" phone call, text or e-mail.

- _____ ☐
- _____ ☐
- _____ ☐

Check as you complete ✓

The most **productive meeting** I was involved in this week and what I hope its impact will be:

_____
_____
_____
_____
_____

> "Someone is sitting in the shade today because someone planted a tree a long time ago."
> - Warren Buffett

Date _____

My intention for this week:

_____

_____

_____

Who I can champion this week:

_____

Three Ways I Can Take Care of **Myself** and **My Students** This Week:

- 1. _____
- 2. _____
- 3. _____

The best three parts of today or "wins" my students had:

Monday:

1. _____

2. _____

3. _____

Tuesday:

1. _____

2. _____

3. _____

Wednesday:

1. _____

2. _____

3. _____

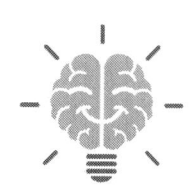

The best three parts of today or "wins" my students had:

Thursday:

1. _____
2. _____
3. _____

Friday:

1. _____
2. _____
3. _____

Something I am especially grateful for this week:

_____
_____
_____

Quote of the Week: (funniest thing a student said, a compliment you were given, something inspirational you read)

Three people I can **thank** or **celebrate** this week - in person, in writing, or by making a "day maker" phone call, text or e-mail.

- _____ ☐
- _____ ☐
- _____ ☐

Check as you complete ☑

The most **productive meeting** I was involved in this week and what I hope its impact will be:

_____
_____
_____
_____
_____

> *"When you judge someone based on a diagnosis you miss out on their abilities, beauty, and uniqueness."*
>
> - Sevenly

Date _____

My intention for this week:

_____

_____

_____

Who I can champion this week:

_____

Three Ways I Can Take Care of **Myself** and **My Students** This Week:

- [ ] 1. _____
- [ ] 2. _____
- [ ] 3. _____

The best three parts of today or "wins" my students had:

Monday:

1. _____

2. _____

3. _____

Tuesday:

1. _____

2. _____

3. _____

Wednesday:

1. _____

2. _____

3. _____

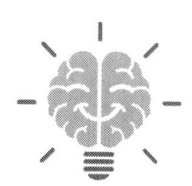

The best three parts of today or "wins" my students had:

Thursday:

1. _____

2. _____

3. _____

Friday:

1. _____

2. _____

3. _____

Something I am especially grateful for this week:

_____
_____
_____

Quote of the Week: (funniest thing a student said, a compliment you were given, something inspirational you read)

Three people I can **thank** or **celebrate** this week - in person, in writing, or by making a "day maker" phone call, text or e-mail.

- _____ ☐
- _____ ☐
- _____ ☐

Check as you complete ✓

The most **productive meeting** I was involved in this week and what I hope its impact will be:

_____
_____
_____
_____
_____
_____

> *"If a child can't learn the way we teach, maybe we should teach the way they learn."*
>
> \- Ignacio Estrada

Date _____

My intention for this week:

_____

_____

_____

Who I can champion this week:

_____

Three Ways I Can Take Care of **Myself** and **My Students** This Week:

- ☐ 1. _____
- ☐ 2. _____
- ☐ 3. _____

The best three parts of today and "wins" my students had:

Monday:

1. _____

2. _____

3. _____

Tuesday:

1. _____

2. _____

3. _____

Wednesday:

1. _____

2. _____

3. _____

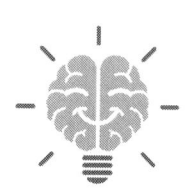

The best three parts of today or "wins" my students had:

Thursday:

1. _____

2. _____

3. _____

Friday:

1. _____

2. _____

3. _____

Something I am especially grateful for this week:

_____
_____
_____

Quote of the Week: (funniest thing a student said, a compliment you were given, something inspirational you read)

Three people I can **thank** or **celebrate** this week - in person, in writing, or by making a "day maker" phone call, text or e-mail.

- _____ ☐
- _____ ☐
- _____ ☐

Check as you complete ✓

The most **productive meeting** I was involved in this week and what I hope its impact will be:

_____
_____
_____
_____
_____

> "Every child you pass in the hall has a story that needs to be heard. Maybe you are the one meant to hear it."
>
> - Bethany Hill

Date _____

My intention for this week:

_____

_____

_____

Who I can champion this week:

_____

Three Ways I Can Take Care of **Myself** and **My Kids** This Week:

- [ ] 1. _____
- [ ] 2. _____
- [ ] 3. _____

The best three parts of today or "wins" my students had:

Monday:

1. _____

2. _____

3. _____

Tuesday:

1. _____

2. _____

3. _____

Wednesday:

1. _____

2. _____

3. _____

The best three parts of today or "wins" my students had:

Thursday:

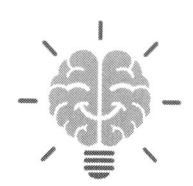

1. _____

2. _____

3. _____

Friday:

1. _____

2. _____

3. _____

Something I am especially grateful for this week:

_____

_____

_____

Quote of the Week: (funniest thing a student said, a compliment you were given, something inspirational you read)

Three people I can **thank** or **celebrate** this week - in person, in writing, or by making a "day maker" phone call, text or e-mail.

- _____ ☐
- _____ ☐
- _____ ☐

Check as you complete ☑

The most **productive meeting** I was involved in this week and what I hope its impact will be:

_____
_____
_____
_____
_____

> *"The kids who need love the most are the ones asking for it in the most unloving ways."*
>
> - Unknown

Date _____

My intention for this week:

_____

_____

_____

Who I can champion this week:

_____

Three Ways I Can Take Care of Myself and My Students This Week:

- [ ] 1. _____
- [ ] 2. _____
- [ ] 3. _____

The best three parts of today or "wins" my students had:

Monday:

1. _____
2. _____
3. _____

Tuesday:

1. _____
2. _____
3. _____

Wednesday:

1. _____
2. _____
3. _____

The best three parts of today or "wins" my students had:

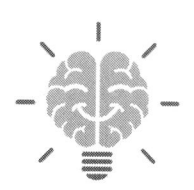

Thursday:

1. _____

2. _____

3. _____

Friday:

1. _____

2. _____

3. _____

Something I am especially grateful for this week:

_____

_____

_____

Quote of the Week: (funniest thing a student said, a compliment you were given, something inspirational you read)

Three people I can **thank** or **celebrate** this week - in person, in writing, or by making a "day maker" phone call, text or e-mail.

- _____ ☐
- _____ ☐
- _____ ☐

Check as you complete ✓

The most **productive meeting** I was involved in this week and what I hope its impact will be:

_____
_____
_____
_____
_____

> "Real education should consist of drawing the goodness and the best out of our own students. What better books can there be than the book of humanity?"
> - Cesar Chavez

Date _____

My intention for this week:

_____

_____

_____

Who I can champion this week:

_____

Three Ways I Can Take Care of **Myself** and **My Students** This Week:

- 1. _____
- 2. _____
- 3. _____

The best three parts of today or "wins" my students had:

Monday:

1. _____

2. _____

3. _____

Tuesday:

1. _____

2. _____

3. _____

Wednesday:

1. _____

2. _____

3. _____

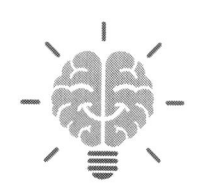

The best three parts of today or "wins" my students had:

Thursday:

1. _____

2. _____

3. _____

Friday:

1. _____

2. _____

3. _____

Something I am especially grateful for this week:

_____

_____

_____

Quote of the Week: (funniest thing a student said, a compliment you were given, something inspirational you read)

Three people I can **thank** or **celebrate** this week - in person, in writing, or by making a "day maker" phone call, text or e-mail.

- _____ ☐
- _____ ☐
- _____ ☐

Check as you complete ☑

The most **productive meeting** I was involved in this week and what I hope its impact will be:

_____
_____
_____
_____
_____

> "A person's a person, no matter how small."
>
> -*Dr. Seuss*

Date _____

My intention for this week:

_____

_____

_____

Who I can champion this week:

_____

Three Ways I Can Take Care of **Myself** and **My Students** This Week:

- [ ] 1. _____
- [ ] 2. _____
- [ ] 3. _____

The best three parts of today or "wins" my students had:

Monday:

1. _____

2. _____

3. _____

Tuesday:

1. _____

2. _____

3. _____

Wednesday:

1. _____

2. _____

3. _____

The best three parts of today or "wins" my students had:

Thursday:

1. _____
2. _____
3. _____

Friday:

1. _____
2. _____
3. _____

Something I am especially grateful for this week:

_____
_____
_____

Quote of the Week: (funniest thing a student said, a compliment you were given, something inspirational you read)

Three people I can **thank** or **celebrate** this week - in person, in writing, or by making a "day maker" phone call, text or e-mail.

- _____ ☐
- _____ ☐
- _____ ☐

Check as you complete ✓

The most **productive meeting** I was involved in this week and what I hope its impact will be:

_____
_____
_____
_____
_____

> *"Correction does much, but encouragement does more."*
>
> - Johann Wolfgang von Goethe

Date _____

My intention for this week:

_____

_____

_____

Who I can champion this week:

_____

Three Ways I Can Take Care of **Myself** and **My Students** This Week:

- [ ] 1. _____

- [ ] 2. _____

- [ ] 3. _____

The best three parts of today or "wins" my students had:

Monday:

1. _____
2. _____
3. _____

Tuesday:

1. _____
2. _____
3. _____

Wednesday:

1. _____
2. _____
3. _____

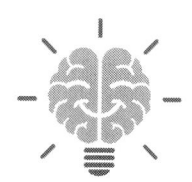

The best three parts of today or "wins" my students had:

Thursday:

1. _____
2. _____
3. _____

Friday:

1. _____
2. _____
3. _____

Something I am especially grateful for this week:

_____
_____
_____

Quote of the Week: (funniest thing a student said, a compliment you were given, something inspirational you read)

Three people I can **thank** or **celebrate** this week - in person, in writing, or by making a "day maker" phone call, text or e-mail.

- _____ ☐
- _____ ☐
- _____ ☐

Check as you complete ☑

The most **productive meeting** I was involved in this week and what I hope its impact will be:

_____
_____
_____
_____
_____

> *"Smile, it is the key that fits the lock of everybody's heart."*
>
> - Anthony D'Angelo

Date _____

My intention for this week:

_____

_____

_____

Who I can champion this week:

_____

Three Ways I Can Take Care of **Myself** and **My Students** This Week:

- [ ] 1. _____
- [ ] 2. _____
- [ ] 3. _____

The best three parts of today or "wins" my students had:

Monday:

1. _____

2. _____

3. _____

Tuesday:

1. _____

2. _____

3. _____

Wednesday:

1. _____

2. _____

3. _____

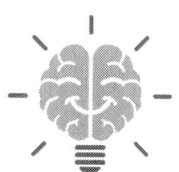

The best three parts of today or "wins" my students had:

Thursday:

1. _____

2. _____

3. _____

Friday:

1. _____

2. _____

3. _____

Something I am especially grateful for this week:

_____
_____
_____

Quote of the Week: (funniest thing a student said, a compliment you were given, something inspirational you read)

Three people I can **thank** or **celebrate** this week - in person, in writing, or by making a "day maker" phone call, text or e-mail.

- _____ ☐
- _____ ☐
- _____ ☐

Check as you complete ☑

The most **productive meeting** I was involved in this week and what I hope its impact will be:

_____
_____
_____
_____
_____

> "Education is the most powerful weapon you can use to change the world."
> - Nelson Mandela

Date _____

My intention for this week:

_____

_____

_____

Who I can champion this week:

_____

Three Ways I Can Take Care of **Myself** and **My Students** This Week:

- 1. _____
- 2. _____
- 3. _____

The best three parts of today or "wins" my students had:

Monday:

1. _____

2. _____

3. _____

Tuesday:

1. _____

2. _____

3. _____

Wednesday:

1. _____

2. _____

3. _____

The best three parts of today or "wins" my students had:

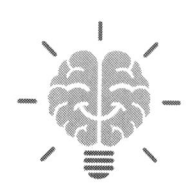

Thursday:

1. _____

2. _____

3. _____

Friday:

1. _____

2. _____

3. _____

Something I am especially grateful for this week:

_____
_____
_____

Quote of the Week: (funniest thing a student said, a compliment you were given, something inspirational you read)

Three people I can **thank** or **celebrate** this week - in person, in writing, or by making a "day maker" phone call, text or e-mail.

- _____ ☐
- _____ ☐
- _____ ☐

Check as you complete ☑

The most **productive meeting** I was involved in this week and what I hope its impact will be:

_____
_____
_____
_____
_____

> *"Try to be a rainbow in someone's cloud."*
>
> \- Maya Angelou

Date _____

My intention for this week:

_____

_____

_____

Who I can champion this week:

_____

Three Ways I Can Take Care of **Myself** and **My Students** This Week:

- 1. _____
- 2. _____
- 3. _____

The best three parts of today or "wins" my students had:

Monday:

1. _____

2. _____

3. _____

Tuesday:

1. _____

2. _____

3. _____

Wednesday:

1. _____

2. _____

3. _____

The best three parts of today or "wins" my students had:

Thursday:

1. _____

2. _____

3. _____

Friday:

1. _____

2. _____

3. _____

Something I am especially grateful for this week:

_____

_____

Quote of the Week: (funniest thing a student said, a compliment you were given, something inspirational you read)

Three people I can **thank** or **celebrate** this week - in person, in writing, or by making a "day maker" phone call, text or e-mail.

- _____ ☐
- _____ ☐
- _____ ☐

Check as you complete ☑

The most **productive meeting** I was involved in this week and what I hope its impact will be:

_____
_____
_____
_____
_____

> *"True teachers are those who use themselves as bridges over which they invite their students to cross; then, having facilitated their crossing, joyfully collapse, encouraging them to create their own."*
>
> - Nikos Kazantzakis

Date _____

My intention for this week:

_____

_____

_____

Who I can champion this week:

_____

Three Ways I Can Take Care of Myself and My Students This Week:

- [ ] 1. _____

- [ ] 2. _____

- [ ] 3. _____

The best three parts of today or "wins" my students had:

Monday:

1. _____
2. _____
3. _____

Tuesday:

1. _____
2. _____
3. _____

Wednesday:

1. _____
2. _____
3. _____

The best three parts of today or "wins" my students had:

Thursday:

1. _____

2. _____

3. _____

Friday:

1. _____

2. _____

3. _____

Something I am especially grateful for this week:

_____

_____

_____

Quote of the Week: (funniest thing a student said, a compliment you were given, something inspirational you read)

Three people I can **thank** or **celebrate** this week - in person, in writing, or by making a "day maker" phone call, text or e-mail.

- _____ ☐
- _____ ☐
- _____ ☐

Check as you complete ✓

The most **productive meeting** I was involved in this week and what I hope its impact will be:

_____
_____
_____
_____
_____

> "Gratitude can transform common days into thanksgivings, turn routine jobs into joy, and change ordinary opportunities into blessings."
>
> - William Arthur Ward

Date _____

My intention for this week:

_____

_____

_____

Who I can champion this week:

_____

Three Ways I Can Take Care of **Myself** and **My Students** This Week:

- ☐ 1. _____
- ☐ 2. _____
- ☐ 3. _____

The best three parts of today or "wins" my students had:

Monday:

1. _____

2. _____

3. _____

Tuesday:

1. _____

2. _____

3. _____

Wednesday:

1. _____

2. _____

3. _____

The best three parts of today or "wins" my students had:

Thursday:

1. _____

2. _____

3. _____

Friday:

1. _____

2. _____

3. _____

Something I am especially grateful for this week:

_____
_____
_____

Quote of the Week: (funniest thing a student said, a compliment you were given, something inspirational you read)

Three people I can **thank** or **celebrate** this week - in person, in writing, or by making a "day maker" phone call, text or e-mail.

- _____ ☐
- _____ ☐
- _____ ☐

Check as you complete ✓

The most **productive meeting** I was involved in this week and what I hope its impact will be:

_____
_____
_____
_____
_____

> *"Watch out for the joy-stealers: gossip, criticism, complaining, faultfinding, and a negative, judgmental attitude."*
>
> *- Joyce Meyer*

Date _____

My intention for this week:

_____

_____

_____

Who I can champion this week:

_____

Three Ways I Can Take Care of **Myself** and **My Students** This Week:

- ☐ 1. _____
- ☐ 2. _____
- ☐ 3. _____

The best three parts of today or "wins" my students had:

Monday:

1. _____

2. _____

3. _____

Tuesday:

1. _____

2. _____

3. _____

Wednesday:

1. _____

2. _____

3. _____

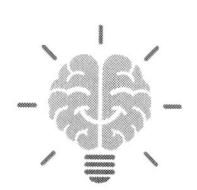

The best three parts of today or "wins" my students had:

Thursday:

1. _____

2. _____

3. _____

Friday:

1. _____

2. _____

3. _____

Something I am especially grateful for this week:

_____

_____

_____

Quote of the Week: (funniest thing a student said, a compliment you were given, something inspirational you read)

Three people I can **thank** or **celebrate** this week - in person, in writing, or by making a "day maker" phone call, text or e-mail.

- _____ ☐
- _____ ☐
- _____ ☐

Check as you complete ☑

The most **productive meeting** I was involved in this week and what I hope its impact will be:

_____
_____
_____
_____
_____

> *"If you don't like something, change it. If you can't change it, change your attitude about it."*
>
> \- Maya Angelou

Date _____

My intention for this week:

_____

_____

_____

Who I can champion this week:

_____

Three Ways I Can Take Care of **Myself** and **My Students** This Week:

- ☐ 1. _____
- ☐ 2. _____
- ☐ 3. _____

The best three parts of today or "wins" my students had:

Monday:

1. _____

2. _____

3. _____

Tuesday:

1. _____

2. _____

3. _____

Wednesday:

1. _____

2. _____

3. _____

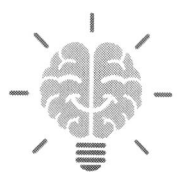

The best three parts of today or "wins" my students had:

Thursday:

1. _____

2. _____

3. _____

Friday:

1. _____

2. _____

3. _____

Something I am especially grateful for this week:

_____

_____

_____

Quote of the Week: (funniest thing a student said, a compliment you were given, something inspirational you read)

Three people I can **thank** or **celebrate** this week - in person, in writing, or by making a "day maker" phone call, text or e-mail.

- _____ ☐
- _____ ☐
- _____ ☐

Check as you complete ✓

The most **productive meeting** I was involved in this week and what I hope its impact will be:

_____
_____
_____
_____
_____
_____

> *"Grades don't measure tenacity, courage, leadership, guts or whatever you want to call it. Teachers or any other persons in a position of authority should never tell anybody they will not succeed because they did not get all A's in school."*
>
> — Thomas J. Stanley

Date _____

My intention for this week:

_____

_____

_____

Who I can champion this week:

_____

Three Ways I Can Take Care of **Myself** and **My Students** This Week:

- ☐ 1. _____
- ☐ 2. _____
- ☐ 3. _____

The best three parts of today or "wins" my students had:

Monday:

1. _____

2. _____

3. _____

Tuesday:

1. _____

2. _____

3. _____

Wednesday:

1. _____

2. _____

3. _____

The best three parts of today or "wins" my students had:

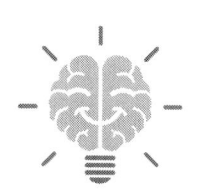

Thursday:

1. _____

2. _____

3. _____

Friday:

1. _____

2. _____

3. _____

Something I am especially grateful for this week:

_____
_____
_____

Quote of the Week: (funniest thing a student said, a compliment you were given, something inspirational you read)

Three people I can **thank** or **celebrate** this week - in person, in writing, or by making a "day maker" phone call, text or e-mail.

- _____ ☐
- _____ ☐
- _____ ☐

Check as you complete ✓

The most **productive meeting** I was involved in this week and what I hope its impact will be:

_____
_____
_____
_____
_____

> "Every child needs a champion- an adult who will never give up on them, who understands the power of connection, and insists they become the best they can possibly be."
>
> - Rita F. Pierson

Date _____

My intention for this week:

_____
_____
_____

Who I can champion this week:

_____

Three Ways I Can Take Care of **Myself** and **My Students** This Week:

- ☐ 1. _____
- ☐ 2. _____
- ☐ 3. _____

The best three parts of today or "wins" my students had:

Monday:

1. _____

2. _____

3. _____

Tuesday:

1. _____

2. _____

3. _____

Wednesday:

1. _____

2. _____

3. _____

The best three parts of today or "wins" my students had:

Thursday:

1. _____

2. _____

3. _____

Friday:

1. _____

2. _____

3. _____

Something I am especially grateful for this week:

_____

_____

_____

Quote of the Week: (funniest thing a student said, a compliment you were given, something inspirational you read)

Three people I can **thank** or **celebrate** this week - in person, in writing, or by making a "day maker" phone call, text or e-mail.

- _____ ☐
- _____ ☐
- _____ ☐

Check as you complete ☑

The most **productive meeting** I was involved in this week and what I hope its impact will be:

_____
_____
_____
_____
_____

> *"If we did all the things we are capable of, we would literally astound ourselves."*
>
> - Thomas Edison

Date _____

My intention for this week:

_____

_____

_____

Who I can champion this week:

_____

Three Ways I Can Take Care of Myself and My Students This Week:

☐ 1. _____

☐ 2. _____

☐ 3. _____

The best three parts of today or "wins" my students had:

Monday:

1. _____
2. _____
3. _____

Tuesday:

1. _____
2. _____
3. _____

Wednesday:

1. _____
2. _____
3. _____

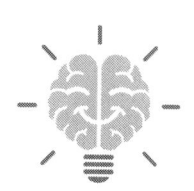

The best three parts of today or "wins" my students had:

Thursday:

1. _____

2. _____

3. _____

Friday:

1. _____

2. _____

3. _____

Something I am especially grateful for this week:

_____
_____
_____

Quote of the Week: (funniest thing a student said, a compliment you were given, something inspirational you read)

Three people I can **thank** or **celebrate** this week - in person, in writing, or by making a "day maker" phone call, text or e-mail.

- _____ ☐
- _____ ☐
- _____ ☐

Check as you complete ☑

The most **productive meeting** I was involved in this week and what I hope its impact will be:

_____
_____
_____
_____
_____

> *"We cannot always do great things. But we can do small things with great love."*
>
> Mother Teresa

Date _____

My intention for this week:

_____

_____

_____

Who I can champion this week:

_____

Three Ways I Can Take Care of **Myself** and **My Students** This Week:

- [ ] 1. _____
- [ ] 2. _____
- [ ] 3. _____

The best three parts of today or "wins" my students had:

Monday:

1. _____

2. _____

3. _____

Tuesday:

1. _____

2. _____

3. _____

Wednesday:

1. _____

2. _____

3. _____

The best three parts of today or "wins" my students had:

Thursday:

1. _____
2. _____
3. _____

Friday:

1. _____
2. _____
3. _____

Something I am especially grateful for this week:

_____
_____
_____

Quote of the Week: (funniest thing a student said, a compliment you were given, something inspirational you read)

Three people I can **thank** or **celebrate** this week - in person, in writing, or by making a "day maker" phone call, text or e-mail.

- _____ ☐
- _____ ☐
- _____ ☐

Check as you complete ✓

The most **productive meeting** I was involved in this week and what I hope its impact will be:

_____
_____
_____
_____
_____

> *"Be somebody who makes everybody feel like a somebody."*
>
> - Kid President

Date _____

My intention for this week:

_____

_____

_____

Who I can champion this week:

_____

Three Ways I Can Take Care of **Myself** and **My Students** This Week:

- ☐ 1. _____
- ☐ 2. _____
- ☐ 3. _____

The best three parts of today or "wins" my students had:

Monday:

1. _____

2. _____

3. _____

Tuesday:

1. _____

2. _____

3. _____

Wednesday:

1. _____

2. _____

3. _____

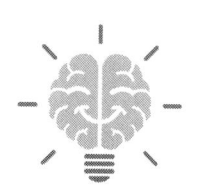

The best three parts of today or "wins" my students had:

Thursday:

1. _____
2. _____
3. _____

Friday:

1. _____
2. _____
3. _____

Something I am especially grateful for this week:

_____
_____
_____

Quote of the Week: (funniest thing a student said, a compliment you were given, something inspirational you read)

Three people I can **thank** or **celebrate** this week - in person, in writing, or by making a "day maker" phone call, text or e-mail.

- _____ ☐
- _____ ☐
- _____ ☐

Check as you complete ☑

The most **productive meeting** I was involved in this week and what I hope its impact will be:

_____
_____
_____
_____
_____

> *"All kids need a little help, a little hope, and somebody who believes in them."*
>
> - Magic Johnson

Date _____

My intention for this week:

_____

_____

_____

Who I can champion this week:

_____

Three Ways I Can Take Care of **Myself** and **My Students** This Week:

- ☐ 1. _____
- ☐ 2. _____
- ☐ 3. _____

The best three parts of today or "wins" my students had:

Monday:

1. _____

2. _____

3. _____

Tuesday:

1. _____

2. _____

3. _____

Wednesday:

1. _____

2. _____

3. _____

The best three parts of today or "wins" my students had:

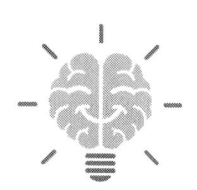

Thursday:

1. _____
2. _____
3. _____

Friday:

1. _____
2. _____
3. _____

Something I am especially grateful for this week:

_____
_____
_____

Quote of the Week: (funniest thing a student said, a compliment you were given, something inspirational you read)

Three people I can **thank** or **celebrate** this week - in person, in writing, or by making a "day maker" phone call, text or e-mail.

- _____ ☐
- _____ ☐
- _____ ☐

Check as you complete ✅

The most **productive meeting** I was involved in this week and what I hope its impact will be:

_____
_____
_____
_____
_____

> "Remember: everyone in the classroom has a story that leads to misbehavior or defiance. 9 times out of 10 the story behind the misbehavior won't make you angry, it will break your heart."
>
> - Annette Breaux

Date _____

My intention for this week:

_____
_____
_____

Who I can champion this week:

_____

Three Ways I Can Take Care of Myself and My Students This Week:

- ☐ 1. _____
- ☐ 2. _____
- ☐ 3. _____

The best three parts of today or "wins" my students had:

Monday:

1. _____

2. _____

3. _____

Tuesday:

1. _____

2. _____

3. _____

Wednesday:

1. _____

2. _____

3. _____

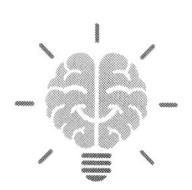

The best three parts of today or "wins" my students had:

Thursday:

1. _____
2. _____
3. _____

Friday:

1. _____
2. _____
3. _____

Something I am especially grateful for this week:

_____
_____
_____

Quote of the Week: (funniest thing a student said, a compliment you were given, something inspirational you read)

Three people I can **thank** or **celebrate** this week - in person, in writing, or by making a "day maker" phone call, text or e-mail.

- _____ ☐
- _____ ☐
- _____ ☐

Check as you complete ✓

The most **productive meeting** I was involved in this week and what I hope its impact will be:

_____
_____
_____
_____
_____

> *"Few things in the world are more powerful than a positive push. A smile. A world of optimism and hope. A 'you can do it' when things are tough."*
>
> \- Richard DeVos

Date _____

My intention for this week:

_____

_____

_____

Who I can champion this week:

_____

Three Ways I Can Take Care of **Myself** and **My Students** This Week:

- [ ] 1. _____
- [ ] 2. _____
- [ ] 3. _____

The best three parts of today or "wins" my students had:

Monday:

1. _____

2. _____

3. _____

Tuesday:

1. _____

2. _____

3. _____

Wednesday:

1. _____

2. _____

3. _____

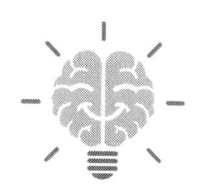

The best three parts of today or "wins" my students had:

Thursday:

1. _____
2. _____
3. _____

Friday:

1. _____
2. _____
3. _____

Something I am especially grateful for this week:

_____
_____
_____

Quote of the Week: (funniest thing a student said, a compliment you were given, something inspirational you read)

Three people I can **thank** or **celebrate** this week - in person, in writing, or by making a "day maker" phone call, text or e-mail.

- _____ ☐
- _____ ☐
- _____ ☐

Check as you complete ✓

The most **productive meeting** I was involved in this week and what I hope its impact will be:

_____
_____
_____
_____
_____

> "I have a very simple philosophy. One has to separate the abilities from the disabilities. The fact I cannot walk, that I need crutches or a scooter or whatever it is, has nothing to do with my playing the violin."
>
> - Itzhak Perlman

Date _____

My intention for this week:

_____
_____
_____

Who I can champion this week:

_____

Three Ways I Can Take Care of Myself and My Students This Week:

- ☐ 1. _____
- ☐ 2. _____
- ☐ 3. _____

The best three parts of today or "wins" my students had:

Monday:

1. _____

2. _____

3. _____

Tuesday:

1. _____

2. _____

3. _____

Wednesday:

1. _____

2. _____

3. _____

The best three parts of today or "wins" my students had:

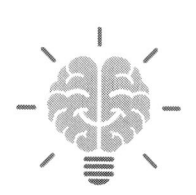

Thursday:

1. _____

2. _____

3. _____

Friday:

1. _____

2. _____

3. _____

Something I am especially grateful for this week:

_____

_____

_____

Quote of the Week: (funniest thing a student said, a compliment you were given, something inspirational you read)

Three people I can **thank** or **celebrate** this week - in person, in writing, or by making a "day maker" phone call, text or e-mail.

- _____ ☐
- _____ ☐
- _____ ☐

Check as you complete ✅

The most **productive meeting** I was involved in this week and what I hope its impact will be:

_____
_____
_____
_____
_____

> "Most of us end up with no more than five or six people who remember us. Teachers have thousands of people who remember them for the rest of their lives."
>
> - Andy Rooney

Date _____

My intention for this week:

_____

_____

_____

Who I can champion this week:

_____

Three Ways I Can Take Care of **Myself** and **My Students** This Week:

- ☐ 1. _____
- ☐ 2. _____
- ☐ 3. _____

The best three parts of today or "wins" my students had:

Monday:

1. _____

2. _____

3. _____

Tuesday:

1. _____

2. _____

3. _____

Wednesday:

1. _____

2. _____

3. _____

The best three parts of today or "wins" my students had:

Thursday:

1. _____

2. _____

3. _____

Friday:

1. _____

2. _____

3. _____

Something I am especially grateful for this week:

_____
_____
_____

Quote of the Week: (funniest thing a student said, a compliment you were given, something inspirational you read)

Three people I can **thank** or **celebrate** this week - in person, in writing, or by making a "day maker" phone call, text or e-mail.

- _____ ☐
- _____ ☐
- _____ ☐

Check as you complete ✓

The most **productive meeting** I was involved in this week and what I hope its impact will be:

_____
_____
_____
_____
_____

> " Knowing that we can be loved exactly as we are gives us all the best opportunity for growing into the healthiest of people."
> - Fred Rogers

Date _____

My intention for this week:

_____
_____
_____

Who I can champion this week:

_____

Three Ways I Can Take Care of Myself and My Students This Week:

- ☐ 1. _____
- ☐ 2. _____
- ☐ 3. _____

The best three parts of today or "wins" my students had:

Monday:

1. _____

2. _____

3. _____

Tuesday:

1. _____

2. _____

3. _____

Wednesday:

1. _____

2. _____

3. _____

The best three parts of today or "wins" my students had:

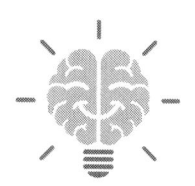

Thursday:

1. _____

2. _____

3. _____

Friday:

1. _____

2. _____

3. _____

Something I am especially grateful for this week:

_____

_____

_____

Quote of the Week: (funniest thing a student said, a compliment you were given, something inspirational you read)

Three people I can **thank** or **celebrate** this week - in person, in writing, or by making a "day maker" phone call, text or e-mail.

- _____ ☐
- _____ ☐
- _____ ☐

Check as you complete ✓

The most **productive meeting** I was involved in this week and what I hope its impact will be:

_____
_____
_____
_____
_____

> *"Each day of our lives we make deposits in the memory banks of our children."*
>
> - Charles Swindoll

Date _____

My intention for this week:

_____

_____

_____

Who I can champion this week:

_____

Three Ways I Can Take Care of Myself and My Students This Week:

- ☐ 1. _____
- ☐ 2. _____
- ☐ 3. _____

The best three parts of today or "wins" my students had:

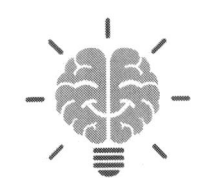

Monday:

1. _____

2. _____

3. _____

Tuesday:

1. _____

2. _____

3. _____

Wednesday:

1. _____

2. _____

3. _____

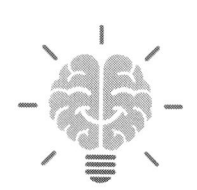

The best three parts of today or "wins" my students had:

Thursday:

1. _____
2. _____
3. _____

Friday:

1. _____
2. _____
3. _____

Something I am especially grateful for this week:

_____
_____
_____

Quote of the Week: (funniest thing a student said, a compliment you were given, something inspirational you read)

Three people I can **thank** or **celebrate** this week - in person, in writing, or by making a "day maker" phone call, text or e-mail.

- _____ ☐
- _____ ☐
- _____ ☐

Check as you complete ✓

The most **productive meeting** I was involved in this week and what I hope its impact will be:

_____
_____
_____
_____
_____
_____

> *"Let us remember: One book, one pen, one child, and one teacher can change the world."*
>
> - Malala Yousafzai

Date _____

My intention for this week:

_____

_____

_____

Who I can champion this week:

_____

Three Ways I Can Take Care of **Myself** and **My Students** This Week:

- ☐ 1. _____
- ☐ 2. _____
- ☐ 3. _____

The best three parts of today or "wins" my students had:

Monday:

1. _____

2. _____

3. _____

Tuesday:

1. _____

2. _____

3. _____

Wednesday:

1. _____

2. _____

3. _____

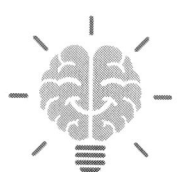

The best three parts of today or "wins" my students had:

Thursday:

1. _____
2. _____
3. _____

Friday:

1. _____
2. _____
3. _____

Something I am especially grateful for this week:

_____
_____
_____

Quote of the Week: (funniest thing a student said, a compliment you were given, something inspirational you read)

Three people I can **thank** or **celebrate** this week - in person, in writing, or by making a "day maker" phone call, text or e-mail.

- _____ ☐
- _____ ☐
- _____ ☐

Check as you complete ☑

The most **productive meeting** I was involved in this week and what I hope its impact will be:

_____
_____
_____
_____
_____

> "The best and most beautiful things in the world cannot be seen or even touched - they must be felt with the heart."
>
> - Helen Keller

Date _____

My intention for this week:

_____

_____

_____

Who I can champion this week:

_____

Three Ways I Can Take Care of **Myself** and **My Students** This Week:

- ☐ 1. _____
- ☐ 2. _____
- ☐ 3. _____

The best three parts of today or "wins" my students had:

Monday:

1. _____

2. _____

3. _____

Tuesday:

1. _____

2. _____

3. _____

Wednesday:

1. _____

2. _____

3. _____

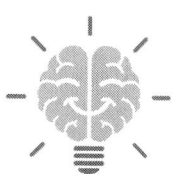

The best three parts of today or "wins" my students had:

Thursday:

1. _____

2. _____

3. _____

Friday:

1. _____

2. _____

3. _____

Something I am especially grateful for this week:

_____
_____
_____

Quote of the Week: (funniest thing a student said, a compliment you were given, something inspirational you read)

Three people I can **thank** or **celebrate** this week - in person, in writing, or by making a "day maker" phone call, text or e-mail.

- _____ ☐
- _____ ☐
- _____ ☐

Check as you complete ✓

The most **productive meeting** I was involved in this week and what I hope its impact will be:

_____
_____
_____
_____
_____

> "Disability is a matter of perception. If you can do just one thing well, you're needed by someone."
>
> - Martina Navratilova

Date _____

My intention for this week:

_____

_____

_____

Who I can champion this week:

_____

Three Ways I Can Take Care of **Myself** and **My Students** This Week:

- ☐ 1. _____
- ☐ 2. _____
- ☐ 3. _____

The best three parts of today or "wins" my students had:

Monday:

1. _____

2. _____

3. _____

Tuesday:

1. _____

2. _____

3. _____

Wednesday:

1. _____

2. _____

3. _____

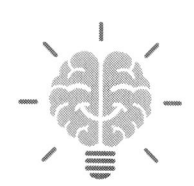

The best three parts of today or "wins" my students had:

Thursday:

1. _____

2. _____

3. _____

Friday:

1. _____

2. _____

3. _____

Something I am especially grateful for this week:

_____
_____
_____

Quote of the Week: (funniest thing a student said, a compliment you were given, something inspirational you read)

Three people I can **thank** or **celebrate** this week - in person, in writing, or by making a "day maker" phone call, text or e-mail.

- _____ ☐
- _____ ☐
- _____ ☐

Check as you complete ✓

The most **productive meeting** I was involved in this week and what I hope its impact will be:

_____
_____
_____
_____
_____

> "Our greatest weakness lies in giving up. The most certain way to succeed is always to try just one more time."
>
> - Thomas Edison

Date _____

My intention for this week:

_____

_____

_____

Who I can champion this week:

_____

Three Ways I Can Take Care of Myself and My Students This Week:

- ☐ 1. _____

- ☐ 2. _____

- ☐ 3. _____

The best three parts of today or "wins" my students had:

Monday:

1. _____

2. _____

3. _____

Tuesday:

1. _____

2. _____

3. _____

Wednesday:

1. _____

2. _____

3. _____

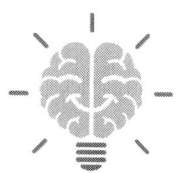

The best three parts of today or "wins" my students had:

Thursday:

1. _____

2. _____

3. _____

Friday:

1. _____

2. _____

3. _____

Something I am especially grateful for this week:

_____

_____

_____

Quote of the Week: (funniest thing a student said, a compliment you were given, something inspirational you read)

Three people I can **thank** or **celebrate** this week - in person, in writing, or by making a "day maker" phone call, text or e-mail.

- _____ ☐
- _____ ☐
- _____ ☐

Check as you complete ✅

The most **productive meeting** I was involved in this week and what I hope its impact will be:

_____
_____
_____
_____
_____
_____

> *"To the world you may just be a teacher, but to your students you are a HERO."*
>
> - Unknown

Date _____

My intention for this week:

_____

_____

_____

Who I can champion this week:

_____

Three Ways I Can Take Care of **Myself** and **My Students** This Week:

- [ ] 1. _____
- [ ] 2. _____
- [ ] 3. _____

The best three parts of today or "wins" my students had:

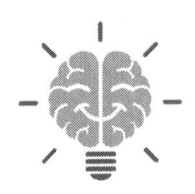

Monday:

1. _____
2. _____
3. _____

Tuesday:

1. _____
2. _____
3. _____

Wednesday:

1. _____
2. _____
3. _____

The best three parts of today or "wins" my students had:

Thursday:

1. _____
2. _____
3. _____

Friday:

1. _____
2. _____
3. _____

Something I am especially grateful for this week:

_____
_____
_____

Quote of the Week: (funniest thing a student said, a compliment you were given, something inspirational you read)

Three people I can **thank** or **celebrate** this week - in person, in writing, or by making a "day maker" phone call, text or e-mail.

- _____ ☐
- _____ ☐
- _____ ☐

Check as you complete ✓

The most **productive meeting** I was involved in this week and what I hope its impact will be:

_____
_____
_____
_____
_____

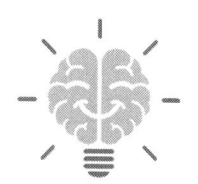

End of Year Reflections

What are some ways that I grew this year?

_____

_____

_____

What was one pleasant surprise this year?

_____

Who did I grow closer to this year that I hadn't expected?

_____

Who is someone who made my year easier this year that I can thank?

_____

_____

What are some ways I can ensure I regroup and recharge this summer?

_____

_____

_____

What are some resources I can look into during break that will make me more effective next year (books, websites, courses)?

_____

_____

_____

In ten years from now, which students will I still remember who brought me the most joy, made me laugh or caused me to stretch the most?

_____

_____

_____

_____

What else will I remember most about this year?

_____

_____

_____

_____

This Year's All Stars

You can use this space to paste in a photo of this year's class or group of colleagues

"A hundred years from now it will not matter what my bank account was, the sort of house I lived in, or the kind of car I drove... but the world may be different because I was important in the life of a child."

- Dr. Forest Witcraft

Good Karma

I thank you from the bottom of my heart for all that you do for children and education. It is an important and noble endeavor to educate minds and build a solid, bright, hopeful foundation for our collective future. At the heart of it all, are the unsung heroes who show up in classrooms every day. The teachers.

Please Help Spread the Love

- If you enjoyed this journal, please consider gifting a copy to a fellow teacher. There are versions available for general education teachers as well as Special Education teachers.
- Also, if you would leave an honest review on Amazon it will help people find this book, and know if it is for them. Every review is so important to me, even if it's just a couple of lines.

You May Also Love

This journal is a companion piece to a book called Positive Mindset Habits For Teachers - 10 Steps to Reduce Stress, Increase Student Engagement and Reingnite Your Passion For Teaching. It's packed with the latest research on positive psychology, exercises and practical advice on how to reduce teacher overwhelm and stress and put passion and joy in your classroom and your life. Find out more at happy-classrooms.com or check it out on Amazon.

Other Versions of This Journal

There are three versions of this journal available. Feedback I received is that it would be fun to have different journal covers for different school years. Also, although the content will be relevant and appeal to all teachers, I am aware that the love heart and floral graphics may not. The academic and darker cover gift copy have more "gender neutral" graphics. Other than the graphics, the content of the journals is the same.

All three versions of the journal are available on Amazon and at HappyHabitsJournals.com

**Gift Edition
Heart Graphics**

**Gift Edition
Regular Graphics**

**Academic Edition
Regular Graphics**

About The Author

"Happier classrooms for teachers and students."

Grace is a public school teacher in Northern California. A self confessed "joy junkie", she is the author of the <u>One New Habit Book Series</u>, as well as <u>Positive Mindset Habits for Teachers.</u>

Grace lived and studied in four countries before making California her home. She stepped away from a successful corporate career when she realized that hanging around young, inquiring minds was a really great way to spend her day.

She holds credentials to teach two foreign languages that she has yet to use, and is also a Certified NLP (Neuro-Linguistic Programming) Practitioner. More importantly, she is a mom to two adult children, twenty third-graders, and one too many cats. They all agree she has a contagious love of learning and a very happy classroom.

Made in the
USA
Lexington, KY